THE REAL
THRIVING

A Guide to Living Happier and Better in every aspect of life

David G. Martinez

Copyright © 2024 by David G. Martinez

INTRODUCTION 5

CHAPTER 1 7

THE INFLUENCE OF MENTALITY 7

CHAPTER 2 12

DEVELOPING ADAPTABILITY 12

CHAPTER 3 19

TAKING CARE OF YOUR HEALTH 19

CHAPTER 4 26

FOSTERING DEEPLY MEANINGFUL RELATIONSHIPS 26

CHAPTER 5 33

FOLLOWING YOUR PURPOSE AND PASSION...................33

CHAPTER 6 40

SETTING AND ACHIEVING OBJECTIVES 40

CHAPTER 7 48

ACCEPTING THANKS...48

CHAPTER 8 54

WELL-BEING FINANCIALLY 54

CHAPTER 9 61

LIVING WITH AWARENESS.......................................61

CHAPTER 10 68

ONGOING DEVELOPMENT AND EDUCATION 68

CONCLUSION 75

INTRODUCTION

The search for happiness is an ongoing desire that cuts across all cultures, ages, and backgrounds in the complex fabric of life. It is a trip filled with ups and downs, triumphs and failures, but at its core, it is a path that offers resilience, fulfillment, and a deep sense of purpose. Greetings and welcome to "Thriving: A Guide to Living Happier and Better," a guide for those who want to genuinely thrive in every aspect of their life rather than just get by.

People everywhere want a life full of joy, meaning, and personal development in a world that frequently moves at an unrelenting pace. This manual explores the ideas and techniques that might enable people to face life's challenges with grace, hope, and a true feeling of thriving—rather than promising a perfect life.

resilience, wellbeing, and the complex web of connections that mold our lives as we begin this life-changing adventure together. We will investigate the significance of meaningful connections, the transformational power of passion and purpose, and how even minor adjustments in viewpoint may have a significant influence on our day-to-day lives.

"Thriving" is a flexible toolset that offers a multitude of tactics and insights that may be customized to your own path rather than a one-size-fits-all answer. It's a call to accept the wonder of ongoing development, practice thankfulness in the face of adversity, and discover delight in the process as well as the final goal.

Therefore, this book is designed with you in mind, regardless of whether you are handling personal crossroads, looking to improve your wellbeing, or just wanting a more fulfilling and happy life. Let's go off on this voyage of self-awareness, fortitude, and flourishing—a path to a better and happier life. Even when the route is not straight, there are always chances for development, relationships, and a fulfilling existence.

May "Thriving" be your dependable ally as you make your way across the landscape of your dreams, giving you the tools you need to pursue your most genuine and joyous self and succeed in the process.

CHAPTER 1

The Influence of Mentality

The lens through which we see the world forms our perceptions, directs our actions, and ultimately determines the course of our lives on the complex terrain of the human experience. This chapter explores the transformational power of mindset—an internal compass that shapes our perception of success and failure, directs our responses to obstacles, and establishes the limits of our personal development and contentment.

1.1 Comprehending the Basics of Mentality

Fundamentally, mentality refers to the profoundly held attitudes and ideas that shape our perspective of ourselves, our skills, and the world around us. The fundamental components of mentality are examined in this part, which also clarifies the differences between growing and fixed mindsets.

Fixed Mindset: People who have a fixed mindset frequently think that their IQ and skill levels are constant. They could shun challenges out of fear of failing and believing that effort is in vain.

Growth Mindset: On the other hand, a growth mindset is defined by the conviction that aptitude and intellect may be enhanced by commitment, diligence, and experience-based learning. People who have a growth mentality like challenges and regard hard work as a means of reaching mastery.

1.2 How Mentality Affects Personal Growth

A person's mindset may significantly influence their resilience, flexibility, and general growth potential. It is a potent accelerator for personal development. This section explores the fundamental effects of mentality on personal growth, looking at how it affects how one responds to failure, how one pursues objectives, and how it is essential to realizing one's potential.

Resilience in Adversity: People who have a growth attitude are more able to bounce back from setbacks. Rather than considering failures as insurmountable barriers, they see them as chances for growth and development.

Pursuit of Goals: The relationship between goal pursuit and mentality is examined. People with a growth mindset approach goals with optimism, seeing work and learning as essential parts of the process.

1.3 Learning and Mindset: Accepting the Process

A person's perspective affects how they approach the lifetime process of gaining information and abilities. Learning is a journey. This section looks into how mentality affects how one approaches learning, how open one is to taking on new challenges, and how deeply one learns from experiences.

Accepting difficulties: People who have a development mentality go out of their way to accept difficulties. They view the process of struggling with complex ideas as a chance to improve their skills and broaden their knowledge.

Learning from Setbacks: One's perspective affects how they interpret and handle setbacks. A growth mindset emphasizes the lessons gained and room for progress, which helps people respond to setbacks with resilience.

1.4 How Mindset Affects Relationships

Beyond personal growth, attitude affects relationships as well, influencing the ways in which people engage with one another. This section examines how mentality affects teamwork, communication, and the development of relationships that are encouraging and goal-oriented.

Growth mentality: People who have a growth mentality are more likely to communicate positively. They actively listen to other points of view and appreciate feedback as a tool for growth, creating an atmosphere that encourages fruitful discussion.

Collaboration and Team Dynamics: A growth mentality fosters productive cooperation in collaborative environments. A growth-oriented team's collaborative spirit is characterized by a readiness to learn from one another, adjust to changing conditions, and recognize group accomplishments.

1.5 Fostering a Growth Mentality: Methods for Transformation

For those who are ready to start, the path toward a development mindset is not only feasible but also attainable. This section offers doable methods for developing and supporting a growth mindset, serving as a road map for anyone looking to change their viewpoints and reach their full potential.

Self-Awareness and Introspection: Developing a development mindset begins with self-awareness. People are urged to examine their prevailing views, identify patterns of stuck thinking, and make a commitment to altering them.

Accepting Difficulties and Educational Possibilities: A growth mindset is based on actively seeking out obstacles and seeing them as chances for personal development. This section offers helpful advice for accepting difficulties and drawing lessons from past encounters.

Building a Positive Inner Dialogue: Our internal language has a big impact on how we think. Techniques for cultivating self-compassion, confronting negative ideas, and creating a constructive internal dialogue are examined.

CHAPTER 2

Developing adaptability

The ability to recover from adversity, or resilience, is essential to wellbeing and personal development. This chapter delves into the complex aspects of resilience and demonstrates how it may be developed, refined, and applied as a potent instrument for overcoming obstacles in life. People can strengthen their mental and emotional toughness by learning the concepts and techniques that support resilience.

2.1 Comprehending Resilience

Rather than being a natural quality, resilience is a talent that can be reinforced and developed over time. This section establishes the foundation by exploring the basic ideas of resilience, breaking it down into its constituent parts, and explaining how it acts as a safeguard against life's unforeseen events.

Adaptability in the Face of Change: One aspect of resilience is the capacity for change adaptation. Resilience is mostly dependent on accepting change as a natural part of life and developing an attitude that supports it.

Emotional Resilience: It has been shown that emotional resilience is a crucial element of total resilience. An individual's ability to manage and control their emotions has a significant role in their ability to handle situations with clarity and serenity.

2.2 Accepting Misfortune as a Growth Catalyst

Adversity is a catalyst for human development rather than just a barrier.   This part explores the transforming potential of accepting adversity, reinterpreting failures as teaching moments, and developing a mentality that views obstacles as stepping stones toward resilience.

Learning from Setbacks: People who are resilient see setbacks as important opportunities for growth. Techniques for drawing lessons from misfortune and applying them to drive one's own development are covered.

Post-Traumatic Growth: This article examines the idea of post-traumatic growth. In addition to helping people overcome obstacles, resilience makes them stronger, wiser, and more equipped to deal with setbacks in the future.

2.3 The Mentality of Resilience

A mentality that guides one's interpretation and response to life's ups and downs is a contributing factor to resilience. The elements of a resilient mentality are discussed in this part, with a focus on the significance of optimism, self-efficacy, and a steadfast conviction in one's capacity to overcome adversity.

Optimism in the Face of Difficulties: Resilience is built on optimism. Maintaining an optimistic mindset when faced with difficulties improves a person's ability to endure and stay hopeful.

Self-Efficacy and Belief in Personal Agency: People who are resilient have a high sense of self-efficacy, or the conviction that they can affect and manage their own circumstances. Building resilience requires cultivating a sense of personal agency.

2.4 Formulating Coping Mechanisms

Building resilience requires knowing how to handle stressors and obstacles in an effective manner. This section examines coping mechanisms that people may use to deal with challenges, control their stress, and develop the emotional resilience necessary to overcome hardship.

Mindfulness and Stress Reduction: It is addressed how to reduce stress and increase resilience in daily life by using mindfulness techniques. Stressors might have a lessening effect on oneself since mindfulness cultivates an awareness of the present.

Effective problem-solving abilities are a prerequisite for building resilience. Techniques for methodically addressing problems, dissecting them into digestible parts, and putting answers into action are discussed.

2.5. Taking Lessons from Failures and Setbacks

Instead of trying to avoid failure, resilience is about growing from it and viewing setbacks as opportunities for improvement. This part explores the skill of growing from mistakes, developing an outlook that views setbacks as chances, and emerging stronger and wiser.

Reflection and Adaptation: People who are resilient exercise reflection, analyzing the causes of setbacks and modifying their strategy as necessary. Resilience is characterized by this continual process of reflection and adaptation.

Developing Emotional Intelligence: Learning from failures is greatly aided by emotional intelligence, which includes self-awareness and empathy. Gaining emotional intelligence makes it easier for someone to face obstacles with wisdom and grace.

2.6 Fostering Emotional Hardiness

The capacity to manage and react to emotions in a healthy and flexible way is known as emotional resilience. This section looks at techniques for developing emotional resilience, encouraging a happy emotional state, and honing the abilities required for efficient emotion management and regulation.

Emotional Awareness and Acceptance: Being more conscious of and accepting of one's feelings is the first step toward building emotional resilience. Techniques for recognizing and embracing feelings without passing judgment are covered.

Healthy Coping Strategies: To deal with stress and emotional difficulties, resilient people use healthy coping strategies. This covers routines like getting enough sleep, working out often, and cultivating positive social networks.

2.7 Developing Social Networks

In difficult circumstances, social networks are an essential source of support. The relationship between relationships and resilience is examined in this section, with a focus on the value of fostering deep ties and asking for help from friends, family, and the community.

Creating a Support System: Resilience is enhanced by actively creating a support system. Techniques for establishing and preserving solid social ties as well as asking for and providing assistance are covered.

The Function of Compassion and Empathy: In social interactions, compassion and empathy promote resilience. Comprehending the significance of empathy in both accepting and giving assistance cultivates a feeling of unity and common humanity.

2.8 Enhancing Physical Welfare

Emotional and mental resilience are closely related to physical well-being. This section examines the relationship between resilience and physical health, offering insights into how self-care, diet, and exercise may help create a strong foundation for overcoming obstacles.

Exercise's Effect on Resilience: Frequent exercise has a significant positive impact on mental and emotional health. The chapter explores the ways in which exercise improves mood, lowers stress levels, and builds resilience in general.

Nutrition and Mental Health: An investigation is conducted into the connection between nutrition and mental health. A healthy, well-balanced diet that feeds the body and brain is essential for resilience.

CHAPTER 3

Taking Care of Your Health

Nurturing well-being becomes essential to living a robust and satisfying life. Physical health, mental clarity, emotional balance, and a feeling of purpose are all components of well-being. This chapter examines comprehensive methods of developing well-being that include activities that lead to a happy and fulfilling existence.

3.1 Total Wellness: Emotion, Body, and Soul

The holistic idea of well-being takes into account how the mind, body, and spirit are all interrelated. This section explores how maintaining a balance between these components might promote resilience and general health.

Mind: Activities like mindfulness, cognitive flexibility, and ongoing learning are important for cultivating mental well-being. A robust and coherent mental state is facilitated by stress management and the cultivation of an optimistic outlook.

Body: Regular exercise, a healthy diet, and enough sleep are the keys to physical well-being. Adopting a healthy lifestyle provides the groundwork for physical resilience, boosts energy levels, and promotes cognitive function.

Spirit: Connecting with something bigger than oneself and discovering a purpose and meaning are aspects of the spiritual dimension. Nurturing the spiritual side leads to a more profound feeling of well-being, whether via values, personal convictions, or a sense of community.

3.2 Mindful Eating for the Body and the Soul

A person's whole well-being is greatly influenced by their diet, which affects their physical and mental health. The necessity of feeding the body and promoting cognitive function is emphasized in this section's exploration of mindful approaches to diet.

Balanced Diet: Essential nutrients for both physical and mental health may be obtained from a diet rich in a range of fruits, vegetables, whole grains, lean meats, and healthy fats.

Mindful Eating: Practicing mindfulness while eating entails enjoying every mouthful, being aware of your body's signals of hunger and fullness, and experiencing the sensory experience of food. Eating mindfully enhances digestion and fosters a positive relationship with food.

Hydration: Maintaining proper hydration is essential to general health. Sufficient hydration is beneficial for maintaining body processes, cognitive performance, and physical toughness.

3.3 Emotional Sturdiness: The Core of Health

A vital element of total wellbeing, emotional resilience affects how people handle and react to life's obstacles. The techniques for developing emotional resilience and creating a pleasant emotional environment are covered in this section.

Emotional Awareness: Acquiring emotional intelligence means being aware of and cognizant of one's own feelings. Resilience and efficient emotional control are based on emotional awareness.

Positive Coping Mechanisms: Developing and utilizing constructive coping strategies, including journaling, painting, or taking up a hobby, enhances emotional health. These systems provide channels for managing feelings and lowering tension.

Creating Emotional Support Networks: Emotional resilience requires fostering a strong social network and asking for help when things are tough. A network of support strengthens coping strategies and fosters a sense of community.

3.4 Restorative Sleep: An Essential Component of Health

A healthy sleep schedule is essential for overall wellbeing, as it affects mental and physical well-being. This section discusses the value of restorative sleep and provides tips for enhancing good sleep hygiene.

Creating a Sleep Schedule: When you stick to a sleep schedule, your body and mind know when it's time to relax. Establishing a consistent bedtime and wake-up time each day aids with sleep-wake cycle regulation.

Establishing a Calm Sleep Environment: Keeping the room cold, reducing light and noise, and providing comfy bedding are all important aspects of creating a calm sleep environment. These elements support sound sleep.

Limiting Screen Time Before Bed: The synthesis of the sleep hormone melatonin can be disrupted by spending too much time in front of displays, such as computers and phones, before going to bed. Better sleep quality is supported when a screen-free period is established before bedtime.

3.5 Developing a Life with Meaning

Resilience and well-being are propelled by a sense of purpose. In addition to discussing the importance of living a purposeful life, this section provides advice for identifying and fostering one's sense of purpose.

Finding Your Core Beliefs: Determining your mission requires an understanding of your unique beliefs. One may clearly see their desired course in life by reflecting on what is really important.

Establishing Meaningful Goals: Meaningful goals and purpose are frequently compatible. A sense of purpose and achievement is created by setting meaningful and achievable goals, which enhances general wellbeing.

Taking Part in Meaningful Activities: Having a sense of purpose is fostered by taking part in activities that are consistent with one's values and objectives. Engaging in meaningful endeavors, whether via employment, hobbies, or community participation, improves well-being.

3.6 Stress Management: Juggling the Demands of Daily Life

Resilience development and sustaining wellbeing depend on effective stress management. The many methods and strategies for managing stress are examined in this section.

Meditation and mindfulness: These techniques help people become more aware of the present moment and relax, which lessens the negative effects of stress on the body and mind.

Exercise: Engaging in regular physical exercise releases endorphins and gives stored tension a release. It is a natural stress-reliever. Including exercise in daily life promotes mental and physical health.

Time management: prioritizing work, establishing reasonable objectives, and keeping a positive work-life balance are all essential components of effective time management. Planning and organizing help people feel more in control and less stressed.

CHAPTER 4

Fostering Deeply Meaningful Relationships

Meaningful relationships are the threads that weave the fabric of a fulfilled life into the tapestry of human experience. The significance of developing real connections with others, the community, and oneself is examined in this chapter. It explores the complexity of interpersonal relationships and provides guidance on building bonds that foster a feeling of purpose, support, and belonging.

4.1 The Significance of Deeply Meaningful Bonds

Meaningful relationships entail a profound sense of comprehension, empathy, and shared experiences in addition to surface-level exchanges. The essence of meaningful connections and their effect on general well-being are examined in this section.

Authenticity and vulnerability: These two qualities are essential to real partnerships. In relationships, being genuine and transparent makes room for greater understanding and builds trust.

Common Ground and Shared Ideals: Shared experiences, interests, or ideals are frequently the foundation of meaningful relationships. Finding points of agreement lays the groundwork for a sense of belonging and connection.

Active Listening and Empathy: Making meaningful relationships requires both active listening and empathy. Relationships are strengthened when people are able to truly hear and comprehend one another's viewpoints and experiences.

4.2 Cultivating Social Bonds

Human well-being depends on social ties, which have an impact on mental, emotional, and even physical health. The methods for fostering and enhancing social ties in a variety of contexts are examined in this section.

Family ties: Sharing experiences, communicating, and offering assistance are all important components of fostering strong ties within the family. Creating a cohesive family unit helps create a support system that endures over time.

Friendships: Mutual support, trust, and common interests are necessary for the development of genuine friendships. Putting forth the time and effort to create and preserve friendships improves social wellbeing.

Community Engagement: Making connections with the larger community helps people feel like they belong and have a purpose. Opportunities for meaningful relationships are created through volunteering, joining local clubs, and taking part in community events.

4.3 Establishing Business Connections

Professional relationships have a significant impact on job satisfaction, teamwork, and personal development. The importance of establishing and preserving strong professional connections is covered in this section.

Effective Communication: Establishing professional connections requires courteous and transparent communication. Open communication encourages cooperation and trust, which improves the working environment.

Mentorship and Networking: Two important tactics for career advancement are establishing professional networks and looking for mentorship. While networks present chances for cooperation and education, mentors give direction and assistance.

Team Building: A great work culture is influenced by strong team dynamics in a professional context. Building a friendly environment, praising accomplishments, and encouraging teamwork all improve professional relationships.

4.4 Building close bonds with others

Whether they are platonic or romantic, intimate connections are the cornerstone of one's overall wellbeing. The processes of developing and maintaining deep connections in personal relationships are examined in this section.

Communication and Emotional Closeness: In close relationships, candid and open communication is essential. Sharing ideas, emotions, and vulnerabilities with mutual respect and trust is a necessary part of developing emotional closeness.

Shared Experiences and Quality Time: Creating shared experiences and spending quality time together strengthens personal bonds. Taking part in activities that you both like helps to build enduring memories and deepen your relationship.

Resolution of Conflicts: Disagreements arise naturally in all relationships. Active listening, empathy, and a cooperative attitude toward problem-solving are all necessary for the development of good conflict resolution techniques.

4.5 Self-Reflection and Self-Compassion as a Means of Self-Connection

It's crucial to have a deep connection with oneself before attempting to connect with others. The significance of self-reflection, self-compassion, and the path toward a more profound comprehension of one's own needs and aspirations are discussed in this section.

Regular self-reflection entails introspection and an examination of one's own values, objectives, and feelings. Self-awareness is aided by journaling, mindfulness, and contemplative activities.

Self-Compassion: The foundation of self-compassion is treating oneself with care and understanding. Positivity and loving relationships with oneself are fostered by recognizing one's talents and embracing one's shortcomings.

Personal Development and Growth: Accepting the path of personal growth entails ongoing education and self-enhancement. Establishing and pursuing personal objectives helps one feel fulfilled and purposeful.

4.6 Technology and Constructive Relationships

In the era of digitalization, technology is crucial to bridging geographical gaps between people. This section examines how technology affects meaningful relationships and provides advice on how to encourage sincere communication in online settings.

Maintaining a Sense of Authenticity and Depth in Relationships: Although technology makes it easier to connect virtually, it is crucial to counterbalance these connections with face-to-face conversations.

Setting limits, controlling screen time, and being deliberate about the caliber of online interactions are all part of mindful technology usage. By practicing mindfulness, technology is used to complement meaningful interactions rather than replace them.

CHAPTER 5

Following Your Purpose and Passion

The threads of passion and purpose combine to form a lively and meaningful pattern in the fabric of a fulfilling life. This chapter delves into the transformational potential of leading a life motivated by a feeling of satisfaction and meaning and examines the tremendous effects of living with passion and purpose.

5.1 Revealing the Strength of Ardor

The motivation that pushes people toward their most important goals is passion. This part examines what passion is all about, how important it is in both personal and professional spheres, and how transforming energy it brings to life in all its forms.

Determining Personal Passion: Determining and comprehending personal passions entails investigating pursuits and interests that elicit sincere zeal and involvement. Passion is a compass that points people in the direction of what really satisfies their souls.

Passion in Professional Pursuits: Bringing one's passion to the workplace helps one feel fulfilled and purposeful. Bringing one's professional goals and hobbies together improves motivation, creativity, and job happiness in general.

5.2 The Core of the Objective

The underlying meaning that provides direction and value to all of life's actions is known as purpose. This section explores purpose in depth, including how it shapes a satisfying life and the significant effects it has on wellbeing.

Clarifying Life Purpose: Determining one's life purpose entails considering one's own ideals, goals, and the constructive contribution one hopes to make to society. A clear purpose statement offers guidance when making decisions and establishing goals.

Purpose in Everyday Actions: Leading a purposeful life entails incorporating intentionality into everyday activities. Every choice you make, no matter how minor, adds to the larger story of a life with meaning. Living with purpose means coordinating one's activities with core beliefs.

5.3 Harmonizing Desire and Objective

There's a potent chemistry when purpose and passion meet. The alignment of purpose and passion is examined in this section, along with how their combination results in a happy and contented existence.

Finding Overlapping Elements: Areas of alignment may be found by looking at the junction of a person's general life goal and their personal interests. Finding the points where these components intersect establishes the basis for a purpose-driven way of living.

Making a Personal Mission Statement: Formulating a personal mission statement expresses the principles, interests, and goals that direct a person's life. A mission statement acts as a continual reminder of what it means to live a life motivated by purpose.

5.4 Overcoming Obstacles with a Purpose

Living with a purpose does not make people immune to difficulties; rather, it offers a strong foundation for

overcoming setbacks. This section looks at how having a purpose may give you strength when things get tough.

Resilience in the Face of Adversity: By offering a more profound comprehension of obstacles, a distinct purpose improves resilience. People with a purpose see failures as chances to improve and gain knowledge.

Motivation in Tough Times: When things get tough, having a purpose may really get you through them. Perseverance and resolve are fueled by the awareness that one's efforts contribute to a more significant and meaningful objective.

5.5 Relationships: Passion and Purpose

Interpersonal relationships are impacted by passion and purpose. This section looks at how leading a life that is in line with your passion and purpose improves relationships and helps you connect with people on a deeper level.

Common Interests and Purposes: In deep and lasting relationships, common interests and purposes frequently coincide with shared values and aspirations. Understanding,

collaboration, and a sense of partnership are all improved by this alignment.

Supporting One Another's Journeys: Relationships are strengthened when loved ones' goals and interests are supported and encouraged. People may confidently pursue their aspirations in a supportive atmosphere.

5.6 Fostering a Sense of Purpose and Passion at Various Stages of Life

Over time, as people go through different phases of life, their passions and purposes change as well. This section looks at how people may develop and modify their goals and interests to fit with evolving circumstances.

Reevaluating and Adapting: It is possible to adjust to shifting priorities, experiences, and life stages by routinely reevaluating one's passions and life purpose. These

components will always be significant and relevant if they are flexible.

Sustained Exploration: Discovering one's interests and purpose throughout life is a dynamic process. Continuous

personal and professional development is facilitated by embracing curiosity and being receptive to new experiences.

5.7 Harmonizing Practicality, Passion, and Purpose

Practical factors are taken into account while making decisions in life, even when passion and purpose offer intrinsic drive. This part addresses the practical issues of daily living while delving into the delicate balance of pursuing one's passion and purpose.

Bringing Passion into the Everyday Normal: People may bring passion into even the most pragmatic and normal areas of life by taking pleasure in the little things, engaging

in hobbies, or bringing in components of their own interests.

Aligning professional decisions with purpose: Finding vocations that align with one's values is a key component of aligning one's professional decisions with one's life purpose. A more satisfying work life is a result of incorporating meaning into the workplace.

CHAPTER 6

Setting and Achieving Objectives

The skill of goal-setting and achievement serves as a compass for people on their path to success and fulfillment in both their personal and professional lives. This chapter delves into the nuances of creating goals that work, the psychology of success, and the transformational impact of realizing dreams.

6.1 The Influence of Objectives

Setting goals is the first step in living an intentional and purposeful life. This section explores the importance of having specific, well-defined objectives, as well as the

psychology of goal formation and how it affects motivation.

Direction Clarity: Well-defined objectives offer a path for both professional and personal development. They provide

guidance, assisting people in making decisions and allocating resources in the direction of their goals.

Motivation and Focus: Setting goals gives one's energy and effort a direction and serves as a strong motivator. They

instill a feeling of urgency and purpose that inspires people to overcome challenges and keep going for their goals.

6.2 Different Goal Types: Long-Term and Short-Term

Setting goals that are both short- and long-term in nature is effective goal-setting. The differences between these kinds of objectives and the tactical method of striking a balance between present needs and long-term ambitions are discussed in this section.

Short-Term Objectives: These serve as stepping stones for longer-term plans. They set clear goals that provide a sense of accomplishment and advancement. Reaching short-term objectives increases confidence and momentum.

Long-Term Objectives: Long-term objectives are lofty ambitions that call for consistent work over a protracted length of time. They give direction and a sense of purpose, influencing the course of a person's career and personal life.

6.3 SMART Framework for Goals

Setting goals is made more organized with the help of the SMART framework, which guarantees that objectives are time-bound, relevant, specific, measurable, and achievable. This section examines every SMART criterion element and how it fits into creating successful objectives.

Particular: Clearly state the objective and the requirements that must be met. Clarity eliminates uncertainty and lays the groundwork for targeted action.

Measurable: Set standards for success and advancement. Measurable objectives enable the tracking of accomplishments and offer concrete markers of success.

Achievable: Make sure the objective is reachable and reasonable. Achievable objectives boost motivation and keep discouragement at bay.

Relevant: Make sure the aim is in line with your beliefs and overall goals. A worthwhile objective advances the overall direction and purpose of a person's life.

Time-bound: Establish a completion date for your goals. A clear deadline fosters responsibility and a sense of urgency, which encourages prompt action.

6.4 Psychology of Goal-Setting: Internal vs. External Motivation

Recognizing the interaction between intrinsic and extrinsic motivation is essential to understanding the psychological components of goal formation. This section examines the ways in which various motivational styles impact goal pursuit and success.

Objectives that are motivated by personal values, emotions, and a sincere desire to better oneself are known as intrinsic

goals. Resilience and enduring commitment are fostered by intrinsic drive.

Extrinsic Motivation: Extrinsic motivation is driven by outside variables like prizes or recognition. Extrinsic motivation works well in the short term, but without an underlying intrinsic desire, it might not be able to maintain long-term commitment.

6.5 Overcoming Difficulties and Failures

Achieving goals rarely follows a straight route; roadblocks and disappointments are unavoidable. This section looks at techniques for overcoming obstacles, developing resilience, and keeping going when things get tough.

Adaptability and Flexibility: When confronted with unforeseen obstacles, embrace adaptability and flexibility.

Continuous progress toward objectives is made possible by modifying tactics and approaches.

Taking Lessons from Failures: See failures as chances for development and learning. Examining difficulties yields insightful information that can improve resilience and guide future decisions.

Creating a Support Network: Nurture a network of friends, mentors, or coworkers. In trying circumstances, a network of support offers perspective, encouragement, and help.

6.6 Honoring Successes and Milestones

Setting and achieving goals requires celebrating every accomplishment, no matter how tiny. The significance of celebrating accomplishments, their psychological effects, and their role in maintaining motivation are all covered in this section.

Positive Reinforcement: Highlighting accomplishments encourages sustained effort and positive behavior. Acknowledging accomplishments boosts confidence and self-worth.

Thought and Gratitude: Give yourself some time to consider the trip and give thanks for all of your hard work. Thinking back on accomplishments strengthens the importance of pursuing goals and cultivates an optimistic outlook.

6.7 Identifying Objectives for Professional and Personal Development

Setting goals that work is applicable to both the personal and professional spheres. This section offers advice on

goal-setting for a variety of areas of life, such as skill development, relationships with others, job progression, and general well-being.

Goals for Career Development: Describe your aspirations for professional development, skill acquisition, and career promotion. Goals for career growth have a positive impact on long-term performance and work happiness.

Establish objectives for your own personal growth, encompassing aspects like relationships, self-improvement, and health. The pursuit of personal improvement objectives leads to a more complete and happy existence.

CHAPTER 7

Accepting Thanks

Gratitude is a colorful thread that interweaves moments of joy, resiliency, and connection in the fabric of a meaningful and full life. This chapter examines the transformational potential of accepting thankfulness, exploring its psychological and emotional advantages, and providing helpful advice on developing an attitude of appreciation.

7.1 What Gratitude Is All About

Gratitude is a deep worldview that affects how people see and engage with the world, not just a transient emotion of gratitude. The core of thankfulness, its foundations in positive psychology, and its effects on general well-being are all covered in this section.

The act of noticing and appreciating the good things in life—the goodness in oneself, others, and the world—is the definition of gratitude.

From the perspective of positive psychology, thankfulness is essential to wellbeing because it fosters pleasant emotions, mental fortitude, and a higher level of life satisfaction.

7.2 Gratitude's Psychological Advantages

Gratitude is a habit that offers long-lasting psychological effects that improve mental and emotional health, going beyond fleeting appreciation. The science of thankfulness and its mental health benefits are examined in this section.

Enhanced Mood and Happiness: Consistent displays of appreciation are linked to higher amounts of happy hormones, which in turn provide a happier and more upbeat attitude toward life.

Decreased Stress and Anxiety: Studies have shown a correlation between gratitude and decreased stress and anxiety. Recognizing the good things in life helps people stay composed and resilient when faced with obstacles.

Better Relationships: People who are grateful typically have more solid and fulfilling relationships. Gratitude strengthens relationships and promotes connection.

7.3 Fostering an Attitude of Gratitude

Gratitude is cultivated through deliberate actions and a change in viewpoint. In order to encourage a more optimistic and thankful mindset, this section examines doable tactics for cultivating appreciation in day-to-day living.

Gratitude Journaling: Consistently recording things for which one is grateful is the goal of keeping a gratitude diary. This exercise cultivates a more cheerful outlook and increases awareness of good events.

Every Day Reflections: Every day, set aside some time to think back on your good fortune, little successes, or acts of compassion. Taking stock of the day's achievements helps you maintain a thankful attitude.

Thanks-Building: When people actively show thanks to one another, whether by words or deeds, connections are strengthened and a positive feedback loop is generated.

7.4: Praise Despite Misfortune

In difficult circumstances, the practice of thankfulness grows especially potent. This section looks at how accepting thankfulness in the face of adversity may strengthen resilience and act as a source of strength.

Finding the Silver Linings: There might be lessons to be learned or positive aspects even under trying circumstances. In the face of hardship, gratitude means looking for the good things, no matter how little.

Mindful Acceptance: Despite obstacles, gratitude is embracing and enjoying life for what it is. Reduction of resistance and facilitation of a calmer mentality are achieved by mindful acceptance.

7.5 Practices and Rituals of Gratitude

The influence of thankfulness on wellbeing is amplified when it is incorporated into regular routines. This section looks at certain rituals and practices for appreciation that people might include in their daily lives.

Practice gratitude-based meditation. Take up techniques that center on appreciation. Calm and inner peace are encouraged by thoughtfully thinking about the things for which to be grateful.

Gratitude Jar: Establish a gratitude jar into which you can periodically add notes of appreciation for good things that have happened to you. This graphic depiction acts as a concrete reminder of all the good things in life.

Writing letters of thanks to people who have positively impacted your life is a great way to show your appreciation. By sharing these letters, one may strengthen relationships and make the other person happy.

7.6 Gratitude and Individual Development

Gratitude is entwined with the path of personal progress. This section examines the relationship between a thankful mentality and self-discovery, resilience, and pursuing a meaningful and rewarding life.

Enhanced Self-Awareness: Embracing the growth path and acknowledging one's own strengths and triumphs is a key component of gratitude. The increased self-awareness serves as a spur for personal growth.

Resilience in the Face of Difficulties: Gratitude builds resilience by encouraging optimism even under trying circumstances. Finding thankfulness in the face of hardship improves coping skills.

CHAPTER 8

Well-Being Financially

A healthy and meaningful life depends on financial wellbeing because it gives people the security and flexibility to follow their dreams. This chapter delves into the fundamentals of financial well-being, practical money management techniques, and the life-changing power of a sound financial mentality.

8.1 Comprehending Financial Well-Being

Financial health includes the capacity to prepare for the future, handle resources sensibly, and feel secure in one's financial situation. It extends beyond the amassing of riches. This section explores the various facets of financial wellbeing and how important it is to overall health.

Financial wellness is defined as a condition of well-being in which people feel in control of their financial situation. It entails wise financial judgments, efficient resource management, and future planning.

Relationship with General Well-Being: Physical, mental, and emotional stability are all correlated with financial wellbeing. A sound financial position lowers stress and raises life happiness in general.

8.2 Establishing a Robust Financial Base

Building a solid financial base is essential to long-term prosperity. The basic ideas that support financial security and stability are examined in this section.

Budgeting: The cornerstone of financial management is the creation and observance of a budget. A well-planned budget allots funds for savings, discretionary expenditures, and necessary costs.

Establishing an emergency fund offers a financial safety net for unforeseen costs. Maintaining a reserve of money lessens stress during trying times and helps avoid financial losses.

Debt Management: Financial wellbeing depends on skillfully controlling and minimizing debt. The secret to financial stability is creating a strategy to pay off high-interest debt and prevent the growth of needless debt.

8.3 Establishing Financial Objectives

A revolutionary step toward financial wellness is setting specific, attainable objectives for your finances. The significance of goal-setting and techniques for coordinating financial goals with personal ambitions are discussed in this section.

Establish clear objectives for your financial future, both short- and long-term. Paying off credit card debt is an example of a short-term objective; retirement or house savings are examples of long-term ambitions.

SMART Goal Framework: When setting financial objectives, consider the SMART criteria (specific, measurable, achievable, relevant, and time-bound). This framework guarantees that objectives are precise and feasible.

8.4 Astute Financial Management Techniques

Adopting tactics that maximize financial resources and foster long-term stability is part of smart money management. This section looks at doable methods for handling money well.

Assets and Savings: Create a methodical savings plan and take into account assets that complement your financial objectives. Long-term financial development is facilitated by judicious investments and compound interest.

Insurance Coverage: Sufficient insurance reduces financial risks and guards against unanticipated catastrophes. This includes health, life, and property insurance.

Tax Planning: You may save a lot of money by being aware of and maximizing your tax methods. Make use of tax-advantaged accounts and consult a professional to ensure thorough tax preparation.

8.5 Financial Literacy and Education

A person with the information and abilities necessary to make wise financial decisions is empowered by financial literacy. The significance of financial education and methods for raising financial literacy are discussed in this section.

Constant Learning: Keep up with market developments, investment opportunities, and personal finance tactics. People who never stop learning are better equipped to adjust to shifting economic conditions.

Seeking Professional Advice: For individualized advice, speak with financial specialists such as advisers or planners. Expert counsel may maximize financial strategy and offer insightful information.

8.6 Getting Past Financial Obstacles

On the financial path, obstacles are unavoidable, but conquering them is crucial to long-term financial wellbeing. This section examines typical financial obstacles and methods for overcoming them.

Job loss or income decrease: To lessen the effects of job loss or income decrease, create backup plans, such as an emergency fund. Investigate different sources of income and ask for assistance as required.

Unexpected Expenses: Life involves unforeseen costs. The financial effects of unanticipated disasters can be lessened by having a flexible budget and an emergency fund.

Managing Debt: Create a methodical approach to control and minimize debt. Give high-interest bills first priority, and if necessary, take debt consolidation measures into account.

8.7 Attaining Economic Independence

When people are financially free, they are able to make decisions that are consistent with their goals and beliefs without feeling weighed down by money. The idea of financial independence is examined in this section, along with methods for achieving it.

Debt Elimination: A vital first step toward financial independence is paying off existing bills. A foundation of financial flexibility and more disposable income is provided by being debt-free.

Investing for Passive Income: Look into ways to make money from your investments, such as interest from bonds, rental income from real estate, and dividends from equities. A stable financial situation is facilitated by passive income.

Create a lifestyle that is in line with your financial objectives and personal beliefs by using lifestyle design. This might entail minimalist living, mindful spending, and deliberate decision-making about one's profession and lifestyle.

CHAPTER 9

Living With Awareness

A transforming way of approaching daily life, mindful living entails developing awareness, appreciating the richness of each moment, and living in the present. This chapter delves into the fundamentals of mindfulness, realistic methods for applying mindfulness to different facets of life, and the significant effects it has on general wellbeing.

9.1: A Comprehensive Guide to Mindful Living

The foundation of mindful living is mindfulness, which is a deliberate state of awareness that entails paying attention to the here and now without passing judgment. The essence of mindful living and its relationship to general well-being are examined in this section.

The definition of mindfulness is the ability to focus attention on the here and now while accepting one's thoughts and feelings without passing judgment. It entails developing an acute awareness of the present moment.

Relation to Well-Being: Living a mindful life is linked to better overall well-being, less stress, and improved emotional control. It entails making the deliberate decision to interact with every moment in an honest and present manner.

9.2 Mindfulness Meditation Practice

Mindfulness meditation, a technique that develops a focused and nonjudgmental awareness, is at the core of mindful living. The foundations of mindfulness meditation and its profound effects on mental and emotional states are examined in this section.

Breath awareness is a common starting point for mindfulness meditation. By concentrating on the breath, one may bring one's attention back to mindfulness by anchoring it in the here and now.

Body Scan Meditation: This type of meditation involves methodically focusing attention on various body areas, developing an awareness of bodily sensations, and encouraging calm.

Love-Kindness Meditation: This type of meditation entails sending compassion and well-wishes to both oneself and other people. Empathy and a sense of connectedness are fostered by this activity.

9.3 Including Mindfulness in Everyday Tasks

Beyond formal meditation, mindful living incorporates daily activities. The practical methods for bringing mindfulness into everyday chores and encouraging attention are covered in this section.

Mindful Eating: Developing awareness of hunger and fullness, relishing every mouthful, and giving your complete attention to the sensory experience of eating are all parts of mindful eating.

Walking with Mindfulness: By focusing on the sensations of movement, the surroundings, and the act of walking itself, regular walks may be transformed into mindful experiences.

Workplace Mindfulness: Incorporate mindfulness into your workplace by taking brief pauses for focused breathing, tackling activities with attention, and giving your complete attention during meetings and conversations.

9.4 Emotional Control and Mindfulness

The influence of mindfulness on emotional regulation is one of its many significant advantages. This section looks at how emotional intelligence and resilience are enhanced by mindfulness practice.

Seeing Emotions Without Passing Judgment: Being mindful entails seeing emotions without passing judgment. People who possess this non-reactive awareness are able to react to emotions in a controlled and deliberate way.

Making Room for Reaction: Being mindful helps to make room for reactions to stimuli. This area gives you the chance to respond deliberately and thoughtfully, as opposed to rashly.

Regular mindfulness practice fosters an accepting and non-reactive attitude toward both pleasant and challenging emotions, which helps to cultivate emotional resilience.

9.5 Conscientious Interaction

Practicing mindful communication entails making self-expression and listening to others more conscious. The foundations of mindful communication are examined in this part, along with how it contributes to the creation of deep connections.

Deep Listening: The first step in mindful communication is deep listening. It promotes comprehension and connection by being really present and paying close attention to the speaker.

Intentional Speech: Develop an awareness of your words and their possible effects before you speak. A conscious communicator uses language that is kind, transparent, and consistent with their beliefs.

Non-Verbal Awareness: Non-verbal clues are also a part of mindful communication. To improve the overall quality of communication, pay attention to your tone of voice, body language, and facial expressions.

9.6 Using Mindfulness to Reduce Stress

A great strategy for reducing stress is mindfulness, which offers a haven from the pressures of an often frenetic and fast-paced society. The contribution of mindfulness techniques to stress management is examined in this section.

Stress Management with Mindful Breathing: Practicing mindful breathing during stressful times can help control the nervous system, which in turn can promote serenity and lessen the physiological effects of stress.

Mindfulness-Based Stress Reduction (MBSR) is an organized program designed to lower stress and improve general well-being. It combines mindfulness meditation with yoga.

Mindful Pause: Throughout the day, people may find moments of respite by pausing, taking a deep breath, and approaching problems more clearly.

9.7 Gratitude and Mindfulness

Gratitude and mindfulness work hand in hand, each strengthening the other's advantages. This section delves into the ways that practicing mindfulness leads to a more profound sense of appreciation.

Present-Moment Awareness: Being mindful requires paying close attention to the present. Because of their increased awareness, people are able to see and value the wealth and beauty in their lives.

Gratitude meditation: As part of mindful living, people can consciously focus on their blessings in order to cultivate a sense of appreciation and satisfaction.

CHAPTER 10

Ongoing Development and Education

The foundation of a happy and meaningful life is constant learning and development. This chapter delves into the

significance of continuous personal and professional improvement, growth mindset cultivation techniques, and the transforming power of a lifetime learning commitment.

10.1 The Importance of Constant Development

A dynamic and deliberate process of development, continuous growth encompasses many facets of existence. This section examines the reasons why continuous development is essential to general wellbeing and personal fulfillment.

Adaptation to Change: People who embrace continual growth are better able to adjust to changing situations in both their personal and professional lives.

Contentment and Goals: By offering chances for self-realization, mastery, and self-discovery, the pursuit of ongoing improvement helps people find their goals and feel fulfilled.

10.2 Fostering a Growth Mentality

The idea of a growth mindset—the conviction that aptitude and intellect may be enhanced by commitment and diligence—lays the foundation for ongoing development. The development mindset's guiding concepts and techniques are examined in this section.

Embracing Challenges: Rather than seeing problems as insurmountable hurdles, people with a growth mindset see challenges as chances for learning and development. Accepting obstacles helps people become resilient and optimistic.

Acquiring Knowledge from Feedback: Having a development mindset entails considering any feedback—positive or constructive—as important data for advancement. Gaining insight from criticism helps one become more self-aware and improve one's talents.

Perseverance and Effort: Developing a development mindset entails appreciating perseverance and effort as necessary ingredients for success. One of the traits of a growth-oriented person is accepting the learning process despite obstacles.

10.3 Curiosity's Place in Constant Development

Exploration, discovery, and a never-ending quest for knowledge are all sparked by curiosity, which is the engine of ongoing progress. The importance of curiosity for both professional and personal growth is discussed in this section.

Inquisitive Exploration: Having an inquisitive mentality means actively looking for new information and experiences. Investigating with curiosity leads to new and unexpected insights and opportunities.

Adaptability: By motivating people to view things with an open mind, curiosity helps people become more adaptable. Having an open mind to other points of view improves one's capacity to adjust to changing circumstances.

Lifelong Learning: A dedication to lifelong learning results from embracing curiosity. Through all phases of life, there is a persistent urge to learn and investigate, which fosters ongoing professional and personal growth.

10.4 Methods for Ongoing Education

A purposeful commitment to continuously learning new things throughout one's life is known as lifelong learning. This section covers practical techniques for bringing lifetime learning into daily practice.

Reading for Self-Education: Make it a habit to read books, articles, and other learning resources on a variety of subjects. Self-education is an effective strategy for lifelong learning.

Online Workshops and Courses: Enroll in online workshops and courses covering a variety of topics. The platforms that make these materials available give easily accessible chances to improve one's knowledge and abilities.

Mentoring and networking: Make connections with a group of people that push and encourage you. Mentorship and networking offer insightful viewpoints and important insights that advance both professional and personal development.

10.5 Enhancement of Skills and Professional Development

The concept of continuous growth also applies to the professional sphere, where career success depends on continued skill development and advancement. The significance of professional growth and methods for acquiring new skills are examined in this section.

Establishing Career Goals: Clearly state your desired path in your career. These objectives act as a road map for career progression, directing the acquisition of the knowledge and expertise required for success.

Skill-Based Training: Determine the essential abilities needed for your line of work and look for specialized training programs. Training focused on skills improves proficiency and advances a person's career.

Attend conferences, seminars, and events tailored to your sector to network. Professional growth requires maintaining up-to-date knowledge of industry trends and networking with other experts.

10.6 Individual Development and Welfare

The development of traits like emotional intelligence, resilience, and a sense of purpose is all included in personal growth. The relationship between personal development and general well-being is examined in this section.

Developing emotional intelligence entails being aware of and in control of both one's own emotions as well as those of others. Effective communication and better relationships are both facilitated by emotional intelligence.

Building Resilience: Developing resilience entails learning how to overcome obstacles and failures. A vital element of emotional health and personal development is resilience.

Clarifying Purpose and Values: A key component of personal development is determining one's own values and coordinating one's activities with those values. A profound sense of fulfillment and significance is fostered by this congruence.

10.7 Juggling Introspection and Execution

Sustaining successful growth requires striking a balance between introspection and action. The relationship between self-reflection and purposeful action to promote continuous development is examined in this section.

Regular Self-Reflection: To evaluate your progress both personally and professionally, set aside time for regular self-reflection. Thinking back on past events, difficulties, and successes yields ideas for new initiatives.

Goal-Setting for Growth: To ensure ongoing growth, establish clear, quantifiable objectives. These objectives direct deliberate activities toward continued growth and function as milestones for accomplishment.

Adapting tactics: Show a willingness to modify your growth tactics in response to criticism and introspection. Adaptability and a readiness to change strategies are elements of continuous improvement.

Conclusion

The search for a purposeful and happy life is an ageless goal on the path through life. A life well lived is not a destination but rather an ongoing journey filled with development, significance, and meaningful relationships. Upon contemplation of the values and methods covered in this manual, we discover that the core of a life well lived is the deliberate development of several aspects that enhance total wellbeing.

mission and passion: finding and pursuing one's mission is essential to living a life effectively. Adopting interests and coordinating activities with a purpose give life significance and provide a compass of fulfillment to help people navigate life's ups and downs.

Personal Development: The pursuit of lifelong learning and development enriches the human experience. Developing a development mindset, valuing inquiry, and continuing education throughout one's life may lead to self-awareness, resiliency, and potential realization.

Wellness of the Mind, Body, and Spirit: Taking care of one's mind, body, and spirit is a key component of holistic well-being. The seamless blending of these dimensions—

from emotional intelligence and mindful living to physical health and spiritual connection—is the hallmark of a well-lived existence.

Meaningful relationships: The fabric of meaningful relationships is what weaves together the strands of a life well lived. A strong sense of fulfillment and belonging may be attained by cultivating a sense of community, exercising empathy, and establishing and maintaining connections.

Financial Wellness: Living a well-lived life means realizing how important financial wellness is in giving one the security and flexibility to follow their dreams. A safe and independent future is a result of goal-setting, prudent resource management, and effective money management.

Gratitude and mindfulness: Adding these two practices to daily life makes each moment more abundant. Through practicing mindfulness, developing appreciation, and enjoying the present moment, people may increase their awareness and strengthen their connection to life's beauty.

Each person creates their own tune in the symphony of these components that speaks to their beliefs, goals, and the ever-changing terrain of their path. A life well lived is not without difficulties, misfortunes, or uncertain times.

Instead, it welcomes these features as chances for development, resiliency, and character improvement.

May these ideas act as beacons of guidance as we draw to an end this investigation of life. The story of a life well lived is a work in progress, molded by intention, decisions, and embracing the moment, whether you are starting out on your path or discovering fresh significance later on.

Ultimately, a life well lived is determined by an internal compass of fulfillment and happiness rather than by just material achievements or social standards. It is evidence of sincerity, kindness, and the unwavering will to make a difference, connect with others, and leave a lasting legacy.

I hope the chapters of your life are full of happiness, purpose, and the fulfillment that comes from knowing that every action you took was a deliberate step toward living a life well lived.